Volume 102 of the Yale Series of Younger Poets

The Earth in the Attic

FADY JOUDAH

Foreword by Louise Glück

811

J86

Yale University Press New Haven and London

Published with assistance from the Mary Cady Tew
Memorial Fund.

Designed by Sonia Shannon.
Set in Electra type by Integrated Publishing Solutions,
Grand Rapids, Michigan.

Printed in the United States of America by Sheridan
Books, Ann Arbor, Michigan.

Library of Congress Cataloging-in-Publication Data
Joudah, Fady, 1971–
The earth in the attic / Fady Joudah ; foreword by
Louise Glück.
p. cm. — (Yale series of younger poets ; v. 102)
ISBN 978-0-300-13430-8 (cloth : alk. paper) —
ISBN 978-0-300-13431-5 (pbk. : alk. paper)
I. Title.
PS3610.O679E25 2008
811'.6—dc22   2007037116

A catalogue record for this book is available from the
British Library.

The paper in this book meets the guidelines for
permanence and durability of the Committee on
Production Guidelines for Book Longevity of the
Council on Library Resources.

10 9 8 7 6 5 4 3 2 1

For my parents
Ahmad & Zarifah

CONTENTS

IV.

Definitions of political poetry are as varied, numerous, and absolute as those of the lyric, with this difference: American poets are eager to define the political in a manner that includes themselves, whereas the lyric will tend to be defined as what the poet has cast off. This was not always so, but in the unstable present, political art seems bold, important, serious, whereas the lyric preoccupations with abiding and insoluble dilemmas seem evasive and frivolous. At the heart of these impassioned realignments is the poet's anxiety lest his art be considered a parlor art: specialized, over-refined, the amusement of privilege.

Underlying these disputes and conversations is a devotion to categories: where there are categories, there are hierarchies.

A problem, of course, is that this language of categories is a language of absolutes, opposing the wholly inward turning gaze to the wholly outward turning, although such distinctions are, rather, a matter of degree. In the fiction of such oppositions, at one extreme is a poetry preoccupied with rarified inner states, with perception, a poetry inclining to the fretfully solipsistic, as though the world were an irritant. And at the other extreme, a poetry that mistakes holding opinions for thinking, a poetry determined to right wrongs, self-consciously immersed in what George Oppen called "the certainties / of place / and of time"—at its worst, bombastic and sentimental, dutifully unbeautiful. But the extremes are rare, and poets both politically alert and spiritually attentive have always existed; I think, in recent years, of Oppen—others will find other examples.

The Earth in the Attic confuses these rituals of classification: Fady Joudah is, in one sense, a deeply political artist (though never an artist who writes to manifest or advance convictions) and in another sense, a luminous aesthete who thinks in nuance, in refinements. He is that strange animal, the lyric poet in whom circumstance and profession (as distinct from will and fashion) have compelled obsession with large social contexts and grave national dilemmas. Under other conditions, one could imagine this elegant austerity, this precision, this dreamy inwardness absorbed entirely in the natural world. But the sky and earth here are the sky and earth of an imperiled country, or the haunted landscapes of a lost homeland. In either case, the present is experienced elegiacally, the atmosphere of legend already permeating it:

The end of the road is a beautiful mirage:

White jeeps with mottos, white
And blue tarps where the dust gnaws
At your nostrils like a locust cloud
Or a helicopter thrashing the earth,
Wheat grains peppering the sky.

For now
Let me tell you a fable:

Why the road is lunar
Goes back to the days when strangers
Sealed a bid from the despot to build
The only path that courses through
The desert of the people.

The tyrant secretly sent
His men to mix hand grenades
With asphalt and gravel,
Then hid the button
That would detonate the road.

These are villages and these are trees
A thousand years old,
Or the souls of trees,
Their high branches axed and dangled

Like lynched men flanking the wadis . . .
                              "Atlas"

"A fable" the poem calls what it re-tells, but the events, the vocabulary, are recent. The landscape is saturated with a narrative violence, but the poem more closely resembles lyric pastoral than contemporary political action poem. Violence has passed, but the earth is changed, its lunar stillness at once beautiful and appalling.

Joudah's position here is that of the outsider, but a particular outsider, his method less interrogation than identification. What in other sensibilities might replicate the colonial gesture, here seems spontaneous, necessary, exact. As an Arab in the West, as a doctor who practices emergency medicine, as a poet writing in English: for a number of reasons, in a variety of situations, Joudah finds himself not at home, not among his people. *The Earth in the Attic* is a book of exile, its biblical resonances less motif than echo. The poet makes of exile not a special case, a perverse snobbery, but rather a metaphor for current psychic reality, as though that reality were indeed displacement, if not geographically, metaphysically: we are adrift, in elemental ways, from the past with all its theoretically useful lessons; the sense of groundedness, of continuity it sustained has vanished. The perception is not new; the treatment is. Of displacement, in these poems, a kind of community is made: "Atlas" ends on a recognition, a tacit gesture of welcome, cautious but potentially inclusive — of the poet, obviously, but also of the reader:

> This blue crested hoopoe is whizzing ahead of us
> From bough to bough,
> The hummingbird wings
>
> Like fighter jets
> Refueling in midair.
>
> If you believe the hoopoe
> Is good omen,
>
> The driver says,
> Then you are one of us.

At the deepest level, the fissure cannot be repaired, though human connection — in friendship, in the ministries of medical aid, in love — does what it can. But the sense of deprivation and longing persist: when Fady Joudah dreams, when he falls in love, nearly always the simile involves the word *home*, a restoration and an arrival. One of the most moving poems, "Proposal," is such a dream:

> I see Haifa
> By my father and your father's sea,
> The sea with little living in it,
> Fished out like a land.

The poem ends:

> And the sea, each time it reaches the shore,
> Becomes a bird to see of the land

What it otherwise wouldn't.
And the wind through the trees
Is the sea coming home.

A longing for community may enact itself as curiosity, even as self-protection recreates distance. Many figures move through these poems, some familial, some strangers, some briefly but intimately known: the men and women who move through a clinic, a population characterized by crisis and transience. In Fady Joudah's quick portraits, each is utterly individual, stark, occasionally comic. These portraits share a refusal of the lingering analytic rumination (which might change them from living people into narcissistic projections) — "Not *why*, but *how*," Joudah says elsewhere, "A humility of science":

One of the drivers ran over the neighbor's ducks
The neighbor demanded compensation
For the post-traumatic stress disorder he accurately anticipates

Do you know what it's like
To drive on roads occupied
By animal farms: you cannot tell
Who killed who or how
Many ducks were there to begin with
                                        "Moon Grass Rain 6"

Today, I yelled at three old women
Who wouldn't stop bargaining for pills they didn't need
One wanted extra
For her grandson who came along for the ride
                                        "Moon Grass Rain 8"

Or this, like many similar moments in the shorter poems:

The carpenter
Dying of cancer in a hospital bed
Saying, god, I know
You've given me misfortune

But when I get up there
There'd better be a damn
Good reason for it,
I've got nothing against trees.
                    "An Idea of Return"

Fady Joudah's gift for swift, telling detail, for image making, manifests in other ways — as observation of nature, as expanded psychological portrait. In their particulars, if not in their movement, the poems seem analogues for photographs. But images here perform a critical psychological (as opposed to aesthetic) function: each image makes a stable referent, an iconic substitute for what is lost. For the same reasons, toward the same result, Joudah's model is less the allegory than the folktale, his language a language in which the anecdotal human past is stored, renewed and affirmed in the retellings. So, too, the chilling testimony of landscape becomes in language fixed, permanent, a means of both affirming and sustaining outrage.

Though an image may *suggest* (in which sense it is not static), it is neither dramatic nor narrative. It follows that poems made of such building blocks move associatively, from image to image, fixed point to fixed point. But in Joudah's work, this movement is neither a buffeted reactiveness (which is passive) nor a meditative rambling (which lacks agenda). In their purposefulness and economy, these lyrics resemble scientific proofs, but proofs written in an utterly direct and human language; in their implicit drivenness, their wish to change the reader as the poet has been changed, the poems acquire a dramatic intensity image making does not usually produce. "Pulse" means to take us beyond naiveté, to equip us with the poet's informed gaze, or the doctor's registering of every detail, collecting evidence (in Hugh Seidman's wonderful phrase). Such seeing and recording have moved far beyond the reeling, self-regarding drama of shock into some more profound, more responsive attentiveness. "Pulse" needs to be read whole, but every section gives indication of its accumulative power:

On the night of the accident
That flipped over the military truck

Cracking many teenage bones, there was a wedding.
The family blazed the air,

Bullets came down
Into the groom's chest.

Last night we heard a *Pop*.
One of us shouted *Wow* in her sleep.

Another, awake and laughing, said:
Here goes the bride

And the dowry: cash
That looks like human remains . . .
                    "Pulse 7"

He fired, they fired, into the air.

By now the slight jerk in the listener's neck
Is a Rilkean gazelle at her water spring.

Toddlers still take off in terror, besieged ·
By calm in the mother's voice.
                    "Pulse 8"

Halimah's mother did not seem aware Halimah was dying.

You should have seen Halimah fight her airlessness
Twisting around for a comfortable spot in the world.

. . . .
. . . Halimah
Died of a failing heart
Early this dawn, her mother, with tears now,

Was on the road, twenty steps past me
Before I turned and found her waiting. . . .
                    "Pulse 12"

Certain of the poems here, notably this sequence, seem located in Dar-
fur — impossible to be certain since the place, or places, are not named. This
is deliberate, not coy, a way of insisting on the representative or paradigmatic
quality of what unfolds. The poems record the survival of the recognizably
human under inhuman conditions — in the hands of a lesser writer, this
would be unreadable, sententious. But what underlies these poems is fury
that the human should be so mercilessly and relentlessly taxed. The tales
Fady Joudah tells are the tales of a very recent present, but a present turned,
absolutely and suddenly, to long ago:

Between what should and what should not be
Everything is liable to explode. Many times
I was told who has no land has no sea. My father
Learned to fly in a dream. This is the story

Of a sycamore tree he used to climb
When he was young to watch the rain.

Sometimes it rained so hard it hurt. Like being
Beaten with sticks. Then the mud would run red.
                    "Sleeping Trees"

The tree is gone — only a fluke that the father isn't. But what he has seen imperils him:

My brother believed bad dreams could kill
A man in his sleep, he insisted
We wake my father . . .

A sense of religious intensity or necessity emanates from these poems, as though, in the absence of the authenticating earth — where home was — only language remains, having to take on the work of both earth and spirit. It is, here, the single means by which tradition and history (the constructs in which the personal is rooted) can be kept alive. Even the most specific and local details have a lyric timelessness. On the page, incident and description are freshly perceived, quotidian; an underlying imperative transforms them into parables, the patina of time already half acquired before the poem is even complete. The tales have an incantatory quality; they more closely resemble spells than gossip. They are the elemental messages of sleep and art, charged with omen:

Say I found you and god
On the same day at the border
Of words, better two late birds than

The stone that hit them. . . .

The poem ends like this:

And in the new country,
Say the hoopoe will still reach us,

Say anything that doesn't wake me
From my morning sleep,
My dreams take too long
And I must finish them.
                    "Love Poem"

The improvisational, let-me-tell-you-a-story *say* of the opening line, the *say* of *just suppose*, becomes, by the end, imperious, a command rooted not in ego-need but in the authority of dream. These are small poems, many of them, but the grandeur of conception inescapable. Fathers and brothers become prophets, hypothesis becomes dream, simple details of landscape transform themselves into emblems and predictions. The book is varied, coherent, fierce, tender: impossible to put down, impossible to forget. It will make itself felt.

In the calm
After the rain has bombed the earth

The ants march out of their shelters
One long frantic migration line

They hit the concrete floor
Of our dining and living

Space then turn into the shadow
The wall makes, a straight angle

To the courtyard wreckage of dirt and gravel:

Did they know the wind
Would airdrop new rations their way?

It's always two or three
Ants locking their horns to the acid end

Over nothing — it seems
More than an impulse,

The debris plenty for all.

"Pulse 10"

—*Louise Glück*

ACKNOWLEDGMENTS

Grateful acknowledgment is made to the editors of the following publications in which the following poems, sometimes in slightly different form, first appeared:

Banipal (London): "Along Came a Spider"
Bat City Review: "Atlas" and "Proposal"
Bellingham Review: "The Name of the Place" and "Anonymous Song"
Beloit Poetry Journal: "Pulse 10" and "Pulse 11"
Crab Orchard Review: "Travel Document" and "Scarecrow"
CutBank: "The Way Back"
Drunken Boat: "Moon Grass Rain"
Hayden's Ferry Review: "Pulse 6," "Pulse 7," and "Sleeping Trees"
The Kenyon Review: "The Tea and Sage Poem"
Literary Imagination: "Pulse 8"
The Massachusetts Review: "Immigrant Song"
Meena: "An Idea of Return" and "Landscape"
New Delta Review: "American Gas Station"
The New Yorker: "The Onion Poem"
Nimrod International: "Pulse 9"
Passages North: "An American Spandrel"
Poetry International: "Pulse 1," "Pulse 4," "Pulse 12," and "Pulse 13"
PoetryMagazine.com: "Love Poem" and "Home"
Prairie Schooner: "Morning Ritual"
Puerto del Sol: "At a Café"
River City: "Additional Notes on Tea" (recipient of the 2004 River City poetry award)
The Texas Observer: "Mother Hair"
Washington Square Review: "Pulse 2"

"Ascension" and "Night Travel" originally appeared in *Iowa Review* in earlier drafts, as part of a longer sequence titled "Night Travel."

"The Tea and Sage Poem" and "Additional Notes on Tea" were translated into French in *Europe* by Jean Migrenne.

"An Idea of Return" and "Landscape" were translated into Arabic in *Meena* (a bilingual magazine) by Khaled Hegazzi.

"Mother Hair" appeared in *White Ink: Poems on Mothers and Motherhood*, edited by Rishma Dunlop.

"Sleeping Trees," "Morning Ritual," "At a Café," and "Additional Notes on Tea" appeared in *Inclined to Speak: An Anthology of Contemporary Arab American Poetry*, edited by Hayan Charara.

"Pulse 10" was featured in *Poetry Daily*.

I would also like to thank Deema Shehabi and Eleanor Wilner for their love and support.

I

Atlas

The end of the road is a beautiful mirage:

White jeeps with mottos, white
And blue tarps where the dust gnaws
At your nostrils like a locust cloud
Or a helicopter thrashing the earth,
Wheat grains peppering the sky.

For now
Let me tell you a fable:

Why the road is lunar
Goes back to the days when strangers
Sealed a bid from the despot to build
The only path that courses through
The desert of the people.

The tyrant secretly sent
His men to mix hand grenades
With asphalt and gravel,
Then hid the button
That would detonate the road.

These are villages and these are trees
A thousand years old,
Or the souls of trees,
Their high branches axed and dangled

Like lynched men flanking the wadis,
Closer now to a camel's neck
And paradoxical chew.

And the villages:
Children packed in a hut

Then burned or hung on bayonets,
Truck tires

Anchoring acacia limbs as checkpoints.
And only animals return:
The monkeys dash to the road's edge and back
Into the alleyways,

And by a doorstep a hawk dives
And snatches a serpent—your eyes
Twitch in saccades and staccatos:

This blue crested hoopoe is whizzing ahead of us
From bough to bough,
The hummingbird wings

Like fighter jets
Refueling in midair.

If you believe the hoopoe
Is good omen,

The driver says,
Then you are one of us.

Pulse

It wasn't over a woman that war began, but it's better
To see it this way, my myth professor loved to say, a man
From the South rumored to extort the bodies of college girls
Into higher grades. My girlfriend of the time told me so —

He was a creep, she
Got an A in the class and liked his joke about religion
As self-mutilation, it was Ramadan then and, O Helen,
I was fasting. I lie awake in a desert night east

Of the Atlantic on the verge of rain, the catapulted grains
Of sand on hot zinc roof, the rustle of leaves, the flap
Of peeling bark on trees whose names I do not know, and where
Would I find a botany guide here. Water flowed

Like a river from the Jabal once.
There were elephant pools, alligator
Streams, and a pond for the devil to speak in human tongues,
All desiccant names now after an earthquake

Shuffled the ground decades ago. It will rain soon,
I'm assured, since nothing has stopped
The birds from migration. All the look-alikes
Are already here: the stork, the heron,

The white flying flowers, the ibis, and the one
That aesthetizes you more.

2.

Nothing holds ground in a poem.
I was with a crane building its nest
When a man from a grass-shrapnel village
Handed me a note that a soldier
Lay in my bed with a bullet
In his thigh . . . I was in the middle
Of tents, mothers in a city
Where each night the donkeys
Are chattering birds after fetching wood
And lugging water.
Then comes tranquility:
The distance from the square
To the quantum of speech:
This one falls out like a parasite
From the gut, a tiny snake. This one
Is the age of lacrimal juice, brief
Like a harvest or a gilded watch
With a cracked face, on the wrist
Of the man who wears
The same suit everyday: in a few days
The body will expel its dead.
In a few days, land will bury the living
And memory will do as it did.

3.

Three sizes of firewood,
One for the skull, two for the spine.

The skull is a woman's,
Pregnant, lactating, or both,
The bundle elegant on her head,
The neck royal, steady, and sometimes

She's among friends, carrying
A child on her back in a cloth sack.

The first spine is a donkey's.
But its back
Is not long enough. And if
The likelihood

Of having your donkey robbed,
Yourself raped or killed upon venturing

Too far, is high,
You would have to wait
For the camel
Owners to come into your market

Of the displaced, they already have
Taken all your cash — A camel
Caravan floating like ocean otters
On the desert floor

Is a hell of a cadence.
The wood they carry is massive.

4.

And in no time
She was up in the mango tree.

He
Only demanded that she

Descend take off
Her dress

And walk home down the orchard path
Naked.

A girl of fourteen
Climbed down

Stepped out
Of her body and gazed at

Her mother the first to reach her
With a shawl:

Whatever they ask
Say he never

Touched you
Whatever happens

He never touched you.

5.

It started with a hand
Grenade in the clutch
Of a boy going down
The road for a stroll.
He fiddled with its ring
As if it were a collar:
There are no canned
Foods here to feed a pet.
In the meandering wadi,
Where the waterholes
Sometimes collapse at the end
Of the parched season, a child
Stood deep in a well with a bucket
Crepuscular except for a smile,
As a dancing parade leading
A bride to her new home
Slipped us in its rhymes:
Khawajah, khawajah . . .
Up the banks a few women
Gathered teargas husks to sell
As spice containers.

6.

Two soldiers, one with his Klash
Limping to the earth behind his back.

A donkey cart led by a boy who stares.

The empty space where a bus,
A can of people, stood in the morning,
The news it flipped three times
And many more were gone.

She loves big automobiles with ornate exotic drawings,
My doctor friend.

I open my French dictionary on Wednesday,
It says, see also Saturday.

A large bird with black wings,
White body, arrives on a branch.

Four women, one with a pot
Of some kind of food you wouldn't eat on her head.

If you come, they will watch you.
You will love it, watching back.

7.

On the night of the accident
That flipped over the military truck

Cracking many teenage bones, there was a wedding.
The family blazed the air,

Bullets came down
Into the groom's chest.

Last night we heard a *Pop.*
One of us shouted *Wow* in her sleep.

Another, awake and laughing, said:
Here goes the bride

And the dowry: cash
That looks like human remains,

You can feel the grains
Of dead skin rolling in your pocket. So handled

The notes, so bandaged, taped and stapled,
Or used as toll for donkey or cow

On the road to stone-thrower mountain:
Where the wretched come from

And the best oranges grow:
Market day, a soldier's favorite.

8.

He fired, they fired, into the air.

By now the slight jerk in the listener's neck
Is a Rilkean gazelle in her water spring.

Toddlers still take off in terror, besieged
By calm in the mother's voice.

The soldier is hush hush.

His proud index against his pursed country lips, a flagpole
Against a cavern that isn't his.

Just as the cows that were stolen today were not his,
The hired rifle not his,

The latrine mall and donkey parking lot for shooting range,
Not his, the wadi and hills, and when

He too would cry for his mother from a shrapnel scratch,
A misfire, a sting in the belly, or dust

In his eyes that blinds him at the hour of five
Each afternoon, pleading for any illness

That sends him away from here, his country.

9.

The sky is yellow today,
Tonight will be so hot you won't sleep.
You stand at the grave of the one
You left last night in the clinic to curfew
And logistics. An old man,
Whose prostate suffocates him, stands
Next to you, he was there
When there was no headcount
Or burial. But today
The sky is yellow.
You've missed the prayer
And the digging. You've made it
For a glimpse of the body in white linen,
Under sweet camphor bark and wood.
Then saplings and mud.
And then the dry sand.

10.

In the calm
After the rain has bombed the earth

The ants march out of their shelters
One long frantic migration line

They hit the concrete floor
Of our dining and living

Space then turn into the shadow
The wall makes, a straight angle

To the courtyard wreckage of dirt and gravel:

Did they know the wind
Would airdrop new rations their way?

It's always two or three
Ants locking their horns to the acid end

Over nothing—it seems
More than an impulse,

The debris plenty for all.

11.

This child
Wears its skin like spandex on the bone.
There's a dry lake fontanelle.
Fontanelle or foramen
Isn't the aesthetic alone, so what
If you threw in Greek or Latin.
Both are openings in the head, one
Is a lack of closure:
This child has a mother
Whose husband was recently killed,
A nascent narrative.
This child was an old man once.
This child heaves its ribs, its eyes
Are cholera eyes, pennies
On a glossy screen, image
In myelin, time
I came off it and told the truth:
I don't feel good today . . .

12.

Halimah's mother did not seem aware Halimah was dying.

You should have seen Halimah fight her airlessness
Twisting around for a comfortable spot in the world.

She would gather all the air she could
In an olympic snatch and curl
Then turn toward her mother's breast to suckle,
But nothing changed,

Neither smell nor taste
Of mother's milk was proof of life. Halimah
Died of a failing heart
Early this dawn, her mother, with tears now,

Was on the road, twenty steps past me
Before I turned and found her waiting.

We walked back toward each other, we met, we
Read verses from the Quran,
Our palms open,
Elbows upright like surgeons

Ready to gown up after scrubbing, the slap
Of rubber gloves before we went our separate ways.

13.

In paradise, hospital beds
Sit under ageless
Mahogany and sycamore that bear
Every kind of fruit.
Hot meals are autumn leaves,
Branches are waitress arms
And also poles for drips.
And birds drop the pills
In your mouth from bills
Of surgical precision.
For Aspirin the swallow.
For Benadryl the nightingale.
No harm befalls you.
The roots will sense your ailment.
The flowers will scan your organs.
Geranium for the spleen,
Poppies for the brain,
And where there's a latrine
A jasmine vine will blossom.

14.

He came, the humanitarian man, and
In the solitude of giving, he befriended
A stray dog as mirror.

Everyday after the long arduous hours
Of the humane, he would come home
To be consoled: the dog

Waiting inside the door,
Wagging and panting, in a rave.
He named him

Something foreign to the population
So as not to offend anyone.
He trained him

To sit on the cheap sofa
One finds in places of conscious exile.
And the dog got to know the front seat of the car,

His tongue licking the air, hair
Blowing, children cheering barefoot.
Then it was time

To make the dog part of his family
Of dogs back home, but the cruel
Government of the wretched refused:

There was no identity card.
And no mirror inside the mirror
Could console the dog, slumped by the door

In hunger strike until it died.
He came, the humanitarian man,
He came and loved, then he went.

15.

It's sixty minutes past the hour.
We are two *khawajahs* running in the first autumn
Downpour, and what else to name the fall
Of desert in the summer months:

Wadis fill with water
And turn the jaundiced earth green,
Green like autumn
A woman told me when I asked what color

Her diarrhea was . . . autumn
Is for chill metamorphosis. No doubt

They think we are mad running in the pelting rain,
The dirt roads for once
Are ours alone, no children
Shouting our titles as if we were prices in an auction.

Maybe, one day, one kid
Will pick up running,
For love handles, say, or for protracted divorce,
Or for the self in the upper percent.

Or maybe another child is a poet
Who will write the two strangers
In one of his famous pieces
For who we really are . . .

And we would call it even.

Proposal

I think of god as a little bird who takes
To staying close to the earth,
The destiny of little wings
To exaggerate the wind
And peck the ground.

I see Haifa
By my father and your father's sea,
The sea with little living in it,
Fished out like a land.

I think of a little song and
How there must be a tree.

I choose the sycamore
I saw split in two
Minaret trunks on the way
To a stone village, in a stone-thrower mountain.

Were the villagers wrong to love
Their donkeys and wheat for so long,
To sing to the good stranger
Their departure song?

I think of the tree that is a circle
In a straight line, future and past.
I wait for the wind to send
God down, I become ready for song.

I sing, in a tongue not my own:
We left our shoes behind and fled.
We left our scent in them
Then bled out our soles.
We left our mice and lizards

There in our kitchens and on the walls.
But they crossed the desert after us,
Some found our feet in the sand and slept,
Some homed in on us like pigeons,
Then built their towers in a city coffin for us . . .

I will probably visit you there after Haifa.
A little bird to exaggerate the wind
And lick the salt off the sea of my wings. I think

God reels the earth in when the sky rains
Like fish on a wire.

And the sea, each time it reaches the shore,
Becomes a bird to see of the land
What it otherwise wouldn't.
And the wind through the trees
Is the sea coming home.

II

Immigrant Song

In the kitchen in the afternoon, peeling oranges and splitting cantaloupe gut,
All that is left is storytelling.

The one-radio, one-coffee-shop village now an almond field
And vacation-brochure ruins besieged by grass.

Everyday around noon a boy on a mule, the men out in the fields,
Bread fresh out of brick-oven, wrist deep in olive oil, elbows dripping.

The one-radio, one-coffee-shop village without an ink-line on paper,
Now spilled like beads out of a rosary.

Not what they would have grown.

We the people in god we trust.

We the people in god we trust everyday around noon a mule.

We the people dream the city: Oooh you give me fever.

Oooh you give me fever so bad I shake like beads out of a rosary.

Fever so bad it must've been malaria.

Hey doctor! You mule-ride away, you cost the rest of harvest.

Hey doctor, the city's a medicine cabinet.

We plant tomatoes, okra, squash instead.

And a fig tree that won't grow in Tennessee frost.

Trees die standing.

One-cantaloupe, one-rosary kitchen.

Mother Hair

My hair, black now, was Achilles hair
When I was a child.
Or maybe Mamluk, maybe Crusader blood,

Though Napoleon could only throw
His hat at the walls of Acre —
Or maybe the ischemic morning

I rode the school bus
Heading for the desert on a field trip —
It doesn't matter. My mother intuited loss

And stroked my head before I waved goodbye.
In the desert
I ate the figs my father had left

By my shoes the night before.
In the desert
Camels are ships

Parting asphalt, and the school bus
Smashed into them and killed
So many children aboard.

When the bus returned
Mothers filled the schoolyard
With wailing,

Smacking their cheeks,
Pulling their hair,
Counting their children.

But there were none missing.
It was only rumor. There was only
Nightfall and my mother, ready,

Wearing black, my hair now,
Maybe Canaanite or Bedouin,
Maybe Fatemah or Zaineb.

The Tea and Sage Poem

At a desk made of glass,
In a glass walled-room
With red airport carpet,

An officer asked
My father for fingerprints,
And my father refused,

So another offered him tea
And he sipped it. The teacup
Template for fingerprints.

My father says, it was just
Hot water with a bag.
My father says, in his country,

Because the earth knows
The scent of history,
It gave the people sage.

I like my tea with sage
From my mother's garden,
Next to the snapdragons

She calls fishmouths
Coming out for air. A remedy
For stomach pains she keeps

In the kitchen where
She always sings.
First, she is Hagar

Boiling water
Where tea is loosened.
Then she drops

In it a pinch of sage
And lets it sit a while.
She tells a story:

The groom arrives late
To his wedding
Wearing only one shoe.

The bride asks him
About the shoe. He tells her
He lost it while jumping

Over a house-wall,
Breaking away from soldiers.
She asks:

Tea with sage
Or tea with mint?

With sage, he says.
Sweet scent, bitter tongue.
She makes it, he drinks.

The Way Back

I know an axe and a turtle's shell.
I know the day I won

A silver watch in school
Then came home with my father

To tell my mother her mother had died.
I know the way

My mother slapped him
And let her nails

Linger. Bleeding,
He smiled to teach me:

We slap whom we love.
I know a boy and a turtle

Each time he held it, it withdrew.
And my aunt was a sea

And two borders removed.
I know the summer she spent waiting

For a visa, sitting in bed, knees
Bent to hold a book she was reading.

No one had told her
Her mother had died.

When she arrived
She smiled and kissed me.

I said nothing. She wailed and
My uncle slapped her once.

I know the sisters wanted
And the boy also wanted.

To see the body
Inside its shell.

There were shovels by the grave.
There was an axe in the garden.

Sleeping Trees

Between what should and what should not be
Everything is liable to explode. Many times
I was told *who has no land has no sea.* My father
Learned to fly in a dream. This is the story
Of a sycamore tree he used to climb
When he was young to watch the rain.

Sometimes it rained so hard it hurt. Like being
Beaten with sticks. Then the mud would run red.

My brother believed bad dreams could kill
A man in his sleep, he insisted
We wake my father from his muffled screams
On the night of the day he took us to see his village.
No longer his village he found his tree amputated.
Between one falling and the next

There's a weightless state. There was a woman
Who loved me. Asked me how to say *tree*
In Arabic. I didn't tell her. She was sad. I didn't understand.
When she left, I saw a man in my sleep three times. A man I knew
Could turn anyone into one-half reptile.
I was immune. I thought I was. I was terrified of being

The only one left. When we woke my father
He was running away from soldiers. Now
He doesn't remember that night. He laughs
About another sleep, he raised his arms to strike a king
And tried not to stop. He flew
But mother woke him and held him for an hour,

Or half an hour, or as long as it takes a migration inward.
Maybe if I had just said it,

Shejerah, she would've remembered me longer. Maybe
I don't know much about dreams
But my mother taught me the law of omen. The dead
Know about the dying and sometimes
Catch them in sleep like the sycamore tree
My father used to climb

When he was young to watch the rain stream,
And he would gently swing.

Resistance

When the thick skinned,
Thin juiced, red
Grapes of summer
Ripen, love and war also ripen.

Their taste and texture
Don't remind the old man
Who prunes them or his wife

Of home. For his part,
He's aware bird and insect
Won't let these strange grapes

Live out their old age
On the vines in peace:
He brings them to the kitchen table

Where they're also beautiful.
And the wife
Smiles in protest.

Because this shortens
Her listening beneath the trellis
On quiet afternoons
To the bumblebees as they sip.

An Idea of Return

I look for your hair and find it
In the night, holding color,
Amber copper,
After so many years inside an envelope.

And I think of the soul
Making speeches hours ago:

The carpenter
Dying of cancer in a hospital bed
Saying, god, I know
You've given me misfortune

But when I get up there
There'd better be a damn
Good reason for it,
I've got nothing against trees.

The carpenter thought I was kind
And searched my nametag for a while

Then said: I know your people.
They're good people, they
Have suffered enough,
And the city is theirs—

The carpenter would be dead by morning.
And why

Did I think your hair
Would have turned white by now?
Like the Mediterranean, frothing at the shore.
And why

You asked for your hair back
Is why I kept it:

Like the city that is only mine
When I'm confused for another.

Love Poem

Say I found you and god
On the same day at the border
Of words, better two late birds than

The stone that hit them.
Say the stone is my death, when we met,
You and I, near the cross

Of the iv pole and fell
In love with the other
Side of the hammer,

The one for removing nails.
Say you will hold me tightly.
Say the pharaoh's daughter

Wanted to play mother,
So the pharaoh tested the divine
With an ember near

The suckling mouth.
Say Moses lisped his promise.
And termites chewed

On Solomon's stick
Until they broke his last repose.
And that you were born in tents

Not made of camel or goat hair,
And our wedding car
Is a Red Cross

Ambulance heading to the border,
And in the new country,
Say the hoopoe will still reach us,

Say anything that doesn't wake me
From my morning sleep,
My dreams take too long
And I must finish them.

Travel Document

It must be like forgetting how to die:
Your grass-grown ruins,
Stonewalls, sadness without eyes.
The body puts on its phantom
Limbs' pain as true account
Of what happens, and a woman
Who's worn the wrong size
Shoes, all her life in flight, her toes
Now crooked, calls flowers by names
You gave then took them back.

If it's the body you want, there is the body
That couldn't return, there is the one
That wouldn't. Sullen
Vengeance. An egg's
Invisible axis rising and sinking
In boiling water, salt
As measure for pickling olives,
Hands without echo's desire
To be heard. Tell me, what else
Is there to say about land?

III

Landscape

I am the distance from birds to Jerusalem
Is a metaphor I like, just because
It follows the laws of calculus,
Much as how the chicken crossed the road:

Not *why*, but *how* —
A humility of science:
In the first instance,
There is a point A, which is fixed,

And a point B, which is in flux,
And *I am* the distance
Between them. In the second,
Two objects collapsing in on each other

In an oblique time,
The car pushing perpendicularly,
The chicken running hysterically
Across the long way out,

Children cheering on both sides
Of the upright road. Which goes along
With a story about my mother
When she was a newborn: They

Ran back to the tent
And found her cooing, next
To a bomb that didn't explode. And so
They named her the amusing one.

I do not say the shelling
Scattered them, I do not say
What Daniel my friend told me: how
He fled across four borders,

And with each
A cerebral malaria that nearly killed him.
The ducks, however,
Get it right from the first time.

The goats, less so, run
Straight ahead of the car for a while,
Before they find their sidestep. The drivers
Slow down, or gun it, and grin.

Scarecrow

The rice field birds are too clever for scarecrows,
They know what they love, milk in the grain.

When it happens, there will be no time to look for anyone.
Husband, children, nine brothers and sisters.

You will drop your sugarcane-stick-beating of plastic bucket,
Stop shouting at birds and run.

They will load you in trucks and herd you for a hundred miles.
Old men will teach you trade with soldiers at checkpoints.

You will give them your spoon, blanket and beans,
They'll let you keep your life. And if you jump off the truck,

The army jeep trailing it will run you over.
Later, they will accuse you of giving up your land.

Later, you will stand in distribution lines and won't receive enough to eat.
Your mother will weave you new underwear from flour sacks.

And they'll give you plastic tents, cooking pots,
Vaccine cards, white pills, and wool blankets.

And you will keep your cool.
Standing with eyes shut tight like you've got soap in them,

Arms stretched wide like you're catching rain.

Anonymous Song

When the shooting began
Everyone ran to the trucks
Grabbed whatever their backs needed
And made for the trucks
Except K

And they begged him to get on
The ones who ran to the trucks
But he refused them all

Later they found him
On the road running
And howling and still
He refused them all
Since he knew
His legend would grow

Then sightings began
He was clothed or naked
Cooking or sleeping
Eating or drinking what
The others gave him

And their begging remained the same
The trucks going loaded
Then coming back empty the same
Until it was forgotten
When K had first lost his mind

Before the shooting started
Or much worse after

One thing for sure
K is real
Safe and sweet especially
Holding a baby to sleep
Or asking for a sip of your Fanta
Or calling out your name from where

You cannot see him

The Name of the Place

There, from a *tukule* built on top of a hundred-years-old
Termite hill, you can see above dry season elephant grass,
You can see a boy and a girl undressing

Then lying down below your vision. The termite hills
Are also sentinels for soccer matches, fertile terraces
For sweet potatoes, rootholds for savanna trees

And what would be a national park had it not been for the hungry
Refugees calling you by skin's name, *chendele*,
Can I please bring a sack of peanuts along for the ride

(To sell, to feed my sister bleeding in a hospital bed,
Please, doctor, one woman said)
And you said: No! Because justice is blind,

Counting down from ten to zero, hands on eyes,
Playing hide & seek on rooftop, a few steps ahead
From where I crouched and saw three girls

Share their tale of pubic hair for the first time:
The one in the middle raised her skirt, the other two
Lowered their jeans, the four of us

Were not caught. We were children then and our night was
Sable tea or Kaaba cloak. The mosque called
For prayer but no one went, our parents talked of a history

By gas lamp where no one wins, and it's true:
Peanuts sell to rich and poor alike,
And once a refugee girl

Watched me write, bouncing
A blown condom that failed
To float into air, and she smiled.

Surviving Caterpillars

They are green stripes dotted black,
Bodies yellow, on branches
Of mango trees. To collect enough

We wait
For the moon to shine tendon white.
They glow

Then suffocate by numbers
In our buckets: the ones on top
Survive but we squeeze

Their heads like bubble wrap,
Separate flesh from gut in a snap,
Toss the body in a skillet. And the moon

Doesn't have to be full:
Just enough to steal
From another's tree,

Get caught and thumb-sliced
Down to cartilage.
Next comes revenge:

An axe in the spine.
And our sunflowers
Taller than our houses

They stoop heavy to the ground.
We grind their seeds into oil.

A little for cooking the caterpillars crisp
To eat or sell at the market for cheap.

Morning Ritual

Every morning, after the roosters
Crow back whatever prayers were passed
Down to them that dawn
From the keeper of their order up in heaven,

I drink my coffee
To the sound of squealing pigs
Being bled to death
In the market up the road—the same market

Where I buy my fresh bread
For my peanut butter and jam. The pigs
Are bled through an armpit wound.
You can see it coming throughout the day before,

Hogs tied sideways to the backs of bicycles,
Tight as a spine, going as far as the border
Where the price is right. You will pass them
On the asphalt to the town I get

The peanut butter and jam from. They know
The bikeways out of nowhere
And suddenly they're alongside your jeep.
I lie: only goats are taken to the border.

The goats are bled differently,
And skinning is harmless after slaughter:
All you do is a vertical skin-slit
Between the shinbone and Achilles tendon,

Stick a thin metal rod
Through it, up the thigh, pull it out
Then blow, mouth to hole,
Until your breath dehisces

Fascia and dermis, reaching the belly:
Your hands
Should even out the trapped air.
Between blowing and tapping

The animal is tight as a drum.
Now the knife that slit the throat.
Who knows
What you'll need skin for.

Moon Grass Rain

1.

Here, shooting stars linger
They give out
A sparkling trail like a cauterized incision

Silver, or amber
If the moon is low and rising red

2.

And the rain melts the roads
And the roads
Can rupture a spleen
Or oust a kidney stone

As for the heart
It needs a beginning
The narrative
Burden of events

3.

"Mize, zey eat mize"
The Frenchman exclaimed with a smile
"Rraized and shipped from za States"

We raise rats! I thought
That's a lot of protein!

"Maize maize!" it was, after our chickens
Have had their fill

4.
She was the only nurse in town before the war
She spoke seven languages and died suddenly
He was a merchant
He's a doorman now and buys us cigarettes

5.
Here we are with love pouring out of every orifice
Here they are dancing
Around the funeral pyre, the corpse in absentia

6.
One of the drivers ran over the neighbor's ducks
The neighbor demanded compensation
For the post-traumatic stress disorder he accurately anticipates

Do you know what it's like
To drive on roads occupied
By animal farms: you cannot tell
Who killed who or how
Many ducks were there to begin with

7.
In the morning, elephant grass moves the way
Mist is visible in the breeze but doesn't dampen the skin

8.
Today, I yelled at three old women
Who wouldn't stop bargaining for pills they didn't need
One wanted extra
For her grandson who came along for the ride

9.
Like lip sores
The asphalt blisters in the rain

And the boys
Fill the holes with dirt and gravel
And broken green branches
Then wait:

No windex. No flowers or newspapers
And gratuity is appreciated

10.
"I have ants in my leg"
And "My leg went to sleep"
Are not the same thing!

The French argue
There is no sleep in a tingling numbness
The symptom of sluggish blood:

I agree. Me too my leg has been anted
And we are learning to reconcile
The dark with the electric

11.
Four days the river runs to the border
Nine days to learn it wasn't the shape
Of your nose that gave you away
And debts are paid off in a-shelter-for-a-day

A pile of wood plus change in your pocket
Is a sack of potatoes and change in another's

12.
No more running long or short distance
The old women
Snicker at me when I pass them by

13.
She was comatose post-partum
And the beekeeper
Bathed her in love everyday

When she recovered I gave up
What he'd promised me for the woman
Who took up nursing their newborn
Since as coincidence would have it
Her name was *Om Assel*—Mother of Honey

14.
The translation of a medical interview
Is not a poem to be written

Come recite a verse from childhood with me
I see you're unable to weep, does love
Have no command over you?

The sea's like the desert
Neither quenches the thirst

15.
Here, dry grass burns the moon
Here, a clearing of grass is a clearing of snakes

16.
And the rain has already been cleansed from the sky
The clinic is empty, soon
The earth will unseal like a jar
Harvest is the season that fills the belly

17.
Here, I ride my bicycle invisible
Except for a crescent shadow and the Milky Way
Is already past

18.
And a mirror gives the moon back to the moon
Home is an epilogue:

Which came first
Memory or words?

Along Came a Spider

On mornings of this refugee settlement,
After the rain falls in stalks
Of mushroom clouds,
The spiders bloom anywhere there's a web-hold
And the earth is like an attic.

By noon, the webs melt from sun or starvation.

And I wonder, how did it really end
Between the prophet
And the holy spider,
The one who had webbed
The cave-mouth shut, quick-
Silver to hide him inside? I wonder

Staring at a black spot suspended in azure sky.

To the left of the spot,
A savanna tree
Whose roots refugees accuse
Of shallow-clutching the earth.
To its right, a termite hill
That cloaked a tree trunk
Splintering the air.

The men, trailing the prophet on horseback,
Knew nothing about entomology,

And did not believe in miracles.
They glanced at the massive web
Sown in the short span of hoof-prints
Still kicking dust in the air north of Mecca,
And thought it had been there for months.

And I wonder all this
While staring at the big black striped spider,

Fanning out its web
Against azure space and insect debris,
It's about 10 feet away
From each boundary, the living tree
And the dead one.

How did the prophet walk out of that cave?

I want to think he negotiated
With the spider first,
Before tearing its home with his camel-stick—
Or did he sit and wait
And watch the spider
Spool its web back inside its belly,
Then ride on camelback
A refugee to Medinah?

This other spider here also does it.

This spider descends,
On a single thread
Hung from a thatched ceiling,
Then hesitates for a while.
Before climbing up the thread,
Reeling it back inside its gut,
And over and over, all night
Sensing place and air.

And in the morning,
After the rain falls
And anywhere is a web-hold

—In glassless windows covered with cloth,
As canopies of sugarcane beds,
Between rows of maize,

Among spines of sunflower,
In mud-brick latrines —

The prophets hide
And the spiders bloom.

IV

An American Spandrel

One of two things, the sweeter of which
Is bitter, uncorrected, held up
By the heat of the ant march
On morning highways and the enuresis of the mind.

The other, the less sweet, the lie
Of the needle, the thread
You wove around me
So softly, this, I give you back a history

Of ideas, a parrot with first words
And no one around to hear it,
An amputee and a rosary
Whispering possibility, impossibility,

One leg walking, the other
Space-walking . . . I am none of those
And neither sweetness. I am
Your favorite night-hour, the one

Your sister always took you away from,
When you two were young and shared the same bed,
One back to the other, watching for ghouls
(For her sake, you said)

Until she slept. And on other nights,
You came home on your bikes,
The house unseen by anyone
Who loved it, and she

Waiting outside for you to walk through ink
Dark rooms and turn on the garage lights.
I am your smile telling me how it was
Just as well, your playing the heroine in need

Of a roof, terrified of witches,
Never having told your sister
About it, how sweet
Secret payback is, and harms no one.

The Onion Poem

Why are there onions the size of swallows in your maple tree?
In the land of cactus wind the one-eyed dwell.

Where is the village whose name holds back the sea?
Caterpillars are for home demolitions in a globe of tents.

Autumn or spring, which is your plumage of choice?
Every empire is a return of the dead.

And Whitman, what would have become of him had you lost the war?
A rooster in rigor mortis pose makes vultures descend.

Is that the easiest pain?
The Hittites veiled their nuclear weapon for as long as they could.

But lilies have rights, iris amendments?
And the bats for rabies are for the urban sunset.

Are you a tiger or a martyr to deforestation?
The genetic map is over the counter.

And the Black Sea is black.
And the Red Sea red.

And the leaves like waves on the pebble shore?
I rake them. My father's garden can use some ash.

Ascension

After fish, we had olive oil ice cream for dessert. The valet brought my steed, only it wasn't my steed: it had topaz eyes and emerald forehead. The valet said: this is your ride from Mecca to Jerusalem, so I kissed my wife goodnight and rode. In the old city, I tied the creature to a rock, took the stairs down to the subway where a throng had gathered around a launch pad to inaugurate me — see me off to god. Between each station was a year of light. At line's end, there was a man with ulcerated skin in a field of aloe. Women sliced their hands instead of onions when I stepped out. An angel, half fire and half ice, was my escort. And by a munificent lotus tree Moses stopped me and advised: *Whatever the decree, ask for less!*

Night Travel

In the first circle of hell
I undressed

A homeless man so drunk
I couldn't tell if he was dying or sleeping.

The one by the wall, on a stretcher,
Met the king east of the river
And the king gave him a horse.

And in bed 9
The weather pilot for Enola Gay.

He said his orders
Were Tokyo first, but bay
Fog was a shelter. Then another

Gasping a ballad.
He'd written it while watching his buddy
In Vietnam die, and he knew

Tonight was his night—I ran
Back to the gate, the guard

Said he'd let me out
Only if I could spell *yum:*

Wrong! he screamed.
It's *y-a* because the *m* is silent!

Condolence

Your best friend died while on holiday
In Casablanca. He'd called the day
Before and left a message
On the answering machine.
The same friend who, years ago,
When your first brother died, dropped by
To honor the dead: we were having a feast
On behalf of the soul and he refused
To eat, but you kept on cooking for each
Visitor who didn't bring his goat or chicken,
A *carnival for the poor, mortality*
With financial ruin, he said,
And the two of you laughed . . .
Then your second brother died.
Checked out hours after a wedding,
A stroke on the commode.
And you busied yourself with that
Andalusian poet you liked so much:
He didn't repeat the same reply
To a condolence twice at his father's funeral.
He was a prince and hundreds of mourners
Had come. You worried about that also
When your last brother died
In the unsayable, vomiting blood
In a hospital without blood
For the elderly. I told you, I spoke
With him on the phone,
That sweet demented brother of yours.
I told you what he said.

Image

My love asked me:
How come the terrorist's eyes seem so kind?
And I thought she was a secret agent
With a wig to hide her medusa hair . . .

My love, whose last name is the same
As an ex-secretary of state's,
Was abandoned by her father
When she was three,

Abused by her mother
Who shot at her and at her two sisters
With an anti-aircraft gun
Until she (the middle child) alighted,

Became a gazelle, swift under the moon . . .
She has long long lashes, the sand stops there.

Bird Banner

A pelican flock flaps as cyclists in the Tour de France do.

They pedal the draft backward, the last one not needing to bat a feather.

Then the rotation: pelicans are a kamikaze of the sea.

And pelican children, when they go hungry, or are
In a feeding frenzy, peck the flesh of their parents' pouches.

High on our honeymoon cliffs
We spot the condor, vizier of wind.

She needs only to thrust her thighs and spread her jewels.

And what kills a condor is not another condor.

Damaged state-of-the-art feathers are famine's sisters: they dance instead.

And whoever wins the dance, blood is rare among equals, they live to old age.

American Gas Station

I never knew Bob.
He was older than some countries
Or a staleness between the teeth and lips,

Nothing the tongue can't sweep away
With few strokes in the middle of mountains
Which are creatures of god.

I had already seen the black-magic-
Marker sign taped to the glass door
Of his gas station,

In the god-damned Sierra,
Where I was grand and American,
Chrysler red and rented, running on empty:

Bob died last night.
And the pumps were locked,
The moon a cataract,

And the man inside, head in one hand,
Waved me away with the other.
I never knew Bob—

But I imagine him bald,
Scalp showing through the mesh of his hat.
I was on vacation,

Tired of killing
Patients and saving them,
And the thought that I might walk for miles

Up mountain roads near dark
Angered me. I admit
What I wanted:

A Coke and a bag of chips.
The key to the toilet after traveling for hours.
I wanted to fall to my knees for oil.

And I admit I have, too many times,
Run on pressurized fumes that pop
Like soda when I finally reach a station.

And because of it,
I was once late for an anatomy test.
And because of it I now

Reset the odometer
Each time I fill my tank,
I measure emptiness.

At a Café

I am still a Muhammadan hunched like a gibbous moon and veiled:
outside, a woman who speaks clearly in order to be heard, right out of the
parlor, nails trimmed and polished, afraid to pop open her diet Pepsi and
damage the cuticles. I use my own teeth-trimmed nails instead, and she
thanks me. We're at a café, not a mosque. And she makes it back safe to
her Jaguar, cell-phone in one hand and a sip in the other, speaking about
the stone in the middle of her heart. The pain doesn't radiate to the left
shoulder, neck, or jaw. The pain never causes her to break out in a sweat.
Which means, I can do nothing about it. And the stone is so huge and
exophytic only her legs and arms are visible. She's a beetle flipped on
her back, stone fungating out of her ribs. Nothing can hide her now, not
even a Trojan horse.

Home

I will know it despite absence of glass
And through women who own shards for mirrors.

A striped wasp will flutter
Like a flag, I will watch it

Come and go building nest,
Or any word other than nest, earth

Grains in mouth spit-glued
Inside the room's wooden window.

Forgetfulness will make me
Strike the nest down in rifle-butt motion.

Forgetfulness, because after violence
Simile blooms in wasp's neural return

To ruins and mouthfuls of grain.
Someone explained this to me once

As a bedtime story. I wanted what
Other powers my wings have.

The thousand feathers that aren't mine
And are whole for no one.

Additional Notes on Tea

In Cairo a boy's balcony higher than a man's deathbed.

The boy is sipping tea,

The view is angular like a fracture.

Surrounding the bed, women in wooden chairs.

They signal mourning with a scream.

Family men on the street run up the stairs and drink raven tea.

On the operating table in Solwezi a doctor watches a woman die.

Tea while the anesthetic wears off,

While the blade is waiting, tea.

The doctor says the woman knows god is sleeping

Outside heaven in a tent.

God is a refugee dreaming of tea.

Once upon a time an ocean married a sea to carry tea around.

Land was jealous.

So it turned into desert and gave no one wood for ships.

And when ships became steel,

Land turned into ice.

And when everything melted, everything tasted like tea.

Once upon a time there was a tea party in Boston.

Tea, like history, is a non sequitur.

I prefer it black. The Chinese drink it green.

Proposal is for Hana el-Sahly.

"Trees die standing" in *Immigrant Song* is a quote my father frequently repeated. Its source is the Palestinian poet Muin Bsiso (1927–1984).

In *Sleeping Trees*, "Who has no land has no sea" is from a poem by Mahmoud Darwish.

Love Poem is for Mona Moussa.

Section 14 of *Moon Grass Rain* combines a quote by the prince poet Abu-Firas al-Hamadani (932–968) with one by the Egyptian poet Amal Donqul (1940–1983).